WINNING!

OTHER BOOKS BY MICHAEL LYNBERG

The Path with Heart
The Gift of Giving

COMPILED AND EDITED
BY MICHAEL LYNBERG

D O U B L E D A Y

New York London Toronto Sydney Auckland

WINNING!

GREAT COACHES AND ATHLETES SHARE THEIR SECRETS OF SUCCESS

A Main Street Book

PUBLISHED BY DOUBLEDAY
a division of Bantam Doubleday Dell Publishing Group, Inc.
1540 Broadway, New York, New York 10036
Main Street Books, Doubleday, and the portrayal of
a building with a tree are trademarks of Doubleday,
a division of Bantam Doubleday Dell Publishing Group, Inc.

Book design by Bonni Leon

Library of Congress Cataloging-in-Publication Data
Lynberg, Michael.
Winning! : great coaches and athletes share their secrets of
success / compiled and edited by Michael Lynberg. — 1st ed.
        p.   cm.
1. Sports—Psychological aspects—Quotations, maxims, etc.
2. Success—Quotations, maxims, etc.   3. Athletes—Quotations.
4. Coaches (Athletics)—Quotations.   I. Title.
GV706.55.L93   1993
796'.01—dc20   92-40069
                                                             CIP

ISBN 0-385-47017-7
Copyright © 1993 by Michael Lynberg
Printed in the United States of America
All Rights Reserved
September 1993
First Edition
1   3   5   7   9   10   8   6   4   2

Once again,
for my parents,
Joanne and Lee

1
WINNING!

Everyone has the will to win, but few have the will to prepare to win.

Bobby Knight

Success is peace of mind in knowing that you did your best to become the best that you are capable of becoming.

John Wooden

I've never known anybody to achieve anything without overcoming adversity.

Lou Holtz

Leadership is getting players to believe in you. If you tell a teammate you're ready to play as tough as you're able to, you'd better go out there and do it. Players will see right through a phony. And they can tell when you're not giving it all you've got. Leadership is diving for a loose ball, getting the crowd involved, getting other players involved. It's being able to take it as well as dish it out. That's the only way you're going to get respect from the players.

Larry Bird

A person always doing his or her best becomes a natural leader, just by example.

Joe DiMaggio

3
WINNING!

He who is not courageous enough to take risks will accomplish nothing in life.

Muhammad Ali

The harder you work, the harder it is to surrender.

Vince Lombardi

I am a winner each and every time I go into the ring.

George Foreman

WINNING!

I have always struggled to achieve excellence. One thing that cycling has taught me is that if you can achieve something without a struggle it's not going to be satisfying.

Greg LeMond

The more difficult a victory, the greater the happiness in winning.

Pelé

Keep fighting for what you desire to achieve. Life is a battle. If people expect otherwise, then constant disappointment occurs. The tougher the job the greater the reward.

George Allen

Lombardi would say, "Listen, I know you can't be perfect. But boys, making the effort to be perfect, trying as hard as you can, is what life is all about." And then he'd say, "Boys, if you'll not settle for anything less than the best, you will be amazed at how much you can do with your lives. You'll be amazed at how much you can rise in the world." I think this consistent unwillingness to settle for anything less than excellence was the greatest thing he left with the people around him.

Bart Starr

The dictionary is the only place where success comes before work. Hard work is the price we must all pay for success.

Vince Lombardi

W I N N I N G !

A competitor will find a way to win. Competitors take bad breaks and use them to drive themselves just that much harder. Quitters take bad breaks and use them as reasons to give up. It's all a matter of pride.

Nancy Lopez

If you're a champion, you have to have it in your heart. You can have the greatest coaches in the world, all the opportunities to play, and the greatest equipment, but if you don't have it inside, you're not going to make it. On the other hand, if you don't have any of those luxuries but you have heart and courage and the guts to go out there and grind it out, then you'll make it.

Chris Evert

There's nothing wrong with finding one aspect of the game and staking your reputation on it. That's how a lot of players made it to the NBA. They're known as just great shooters, great passers, great rebounders, or great defenders. But to be known as an all-around player, I knew I had to be sound in every part of the game. It didn't make sense to work so hard on one part of the game I could already do well, then forget about working on my weaknesses. Dad said my opponents would always find my weaknesses, and that it wouldn't take long, at any level, for them to start exploiting me. He said my weaknesses would stand out like a neon sign. If I couldn't dribble with my left hand or if I had the habit of being lazy on defense, everybody would know it. He told me that in basketball I couldn't hide.

Magic Johnson

WINNING!

Wherever I've been, as long as someone was paying my salary, I've tried to give a dollar and twenty-five cents in work for every dollar paid me. In other words, I might not win, but the effort would be there.

Casey Stengel

My baseball career spanned almost five decades—from 1925 to 1973, count them—and in all that time I never had a boss call me upstairs so that he could congratulate me for losing like a gentleman. When you're playing for money, winning is the only thing that matters. Show me a good loser in professional sports, and I'll show you an idiot. Show me a sportsman, and I'll show you a player I'm looking to trade.

Leo Durocher

WINNING!

When I was a kid in Louisville I had a job sacking groceries. I found a secondhand but really sharp bicycle I just had to have. It was blue and beautiful. I didn't make much money at the grocery but I finally saved up enough to get that secondhand bike. I parked it behind the store, proud and happy. I worked hard for it. Then somebody stole it. Just about broke my heart. I walked all over Louisville that summer, looking for that bicycle. I walked and looked, looked and walked. Never found it to this day. But every time I got into the ring, I looked across at the other fighter and I told myself, "Hey, that's the guy that stole my bicycle!"

Muhammad Ali

WINNING!

Confidence is a lot of this game or any game. If you don't think you can, you won't.

Jerry West

What you're thinking, what shape your mind is in, is what makes the biggest difference of all.

Willie Mays

I always thought I could play pro ball. I had confidence in my ability. You have to. If you don't, who will?

Johnny Unitas

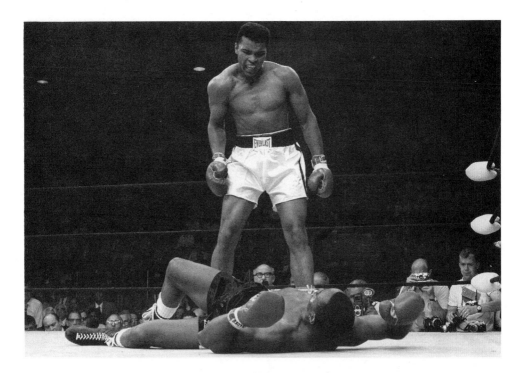

WINNING!

I could not retreat from a challenge. If the chance was there and if—no matter how difficult it appeared—it meant winning, I was going to take it. It was the "sweetness" of the risk that I remembered, and not its dangers. You must play boldly to win.

Arnold Palmer

Aggressive play is a vital asset of the world's greatest golfers. However, it's even more important to the average player. Attack this game in a bold, confident, and determined way, and you'll make a giant leap toward realizing your full potential as a player.

Greg Norman

WINNING!

Be quick, but never hurry.

John Wooden

When all is said and done, as a rule, more is said than done.

Lou Holtz

Luck is the residue of design.

Branch Rickey

One day, during the 1983 Stanley Cup, we'd just lost Game Three and we were down three games to none. We were practicing and afterward my dad came down to me and said, "Why did you practice today?" "Because we had to," I said. "Everybody had to." "Well you shouldn't have. You just wasted your time and theirs. You didn't give an effort."

That was the last we talked about it until later that summer. We were at my grandmother's house and she was out in the sun working in the garden, and my dad comes up to me and says, "Look at that, seventy-nine and she's still working hard and you're twenty-three and when you're in the Stanley Cup finals, you won't even practice!"

Ever since then, the highest compliment you can pay me is to say that I work hard every day, that I never dog it.

Wayne Gretzky

WINNING!

The mark of a great player is in his ability to come back. The great champions have all come back from defeat.

Sam Snead

There aren't any tricks. It's hard work and pain and loneliness. But you can come back. That's what I want everybody to know—you can come back.

Gale Sayers

Achievement is difficult. It requires enormous effort. Those who can work through the struggle are the ones who are going to be successful.

Jackie Joyner-Kersee

What is the single most important quality in a tennis champion? I would have to say *desire,* staying in there and winning matches when you are not playing that well. It comes down to the mental aspect. All champions have that quality. They don't give up, they dig into something extra. People can sense that and see that. That is a necessity if you really want to be considered a champion.

John McEnroe

Most coaches hate preventable mistakes as much as I did. Somebody asked Don Shula if it wasn't a waste of time bothering to correct a small flaw. "What's a small flaw?" Don wanted to know.

John Madden

Whatever your goal in life, be proud of every day that you are able to work in that direction.

Chris Evert

You build a successful life a day at a time.

Lou Holtz

Don't measure yourself by what you have accomplished, but by what you should have accomplished with your ability.

John Wooden

WINNING!

There's nothing wrong with wanting to win. There's nothing wrong with grinding your guts to do everything you can to make it happen.

There's something definitely wrong, though, when you take it to the point where winning becomes an obsession and hazardous to your health or the well-being of your family. That's when the urgency to win crosses over the line of sanity. That's when winning actually becomes a disease.

The trick is to realize that after giving your best, there's nothing more to give. There's no shame in losing. As long as you gave it your best. Win or lose, the game is finished. It's over. It's time to forget and prepare for the next one.

Sparky Anderson

WINNING!

Winning isn't everything—but making the effort to win is.

Vince Lombardi

Losing is no disgrace if you've given your best.

Jim Palmer

You can win and still not succeed, still not achieve what you should. And you can lose without really failing at all.

Bobby Knight

Winning is fun and it's the American way. But for kids at a young age, athletics should be stressed for the pleasure of participating. If a child is provided with the proper environment he will begin to learn the lessons of athletics which are useful in everyday life—working as a team, self-discipline and personal sacrifice. But if he's thrown against must-win pressures, athletics will become a negative experience and he soon will drop out. If a kid loses, he shouldn't worry about it, but learn from the experience.

Roger Staubach

What's important is that kids discover baseball is fun—and that it gets to be more fun as you get better at it.

Mickey Mantle

The role of my parents was perfect. They were helpful but never interfered with my tennis. I was obviously crazy about tennis from the beginning and they gave assistance all the time but never told me what to do, when to practice, when to play tournaments. It's like taking piano lessons when you're young. If they had told me I had to practice four hours a day and pushed it down my throat, I would have quit tennis.

Bjorn Borg

A lot of parents think kids ought to learn responsibility from work, and I've always said, "Baloney." Kids learn leadership and organization from games, from having fun.

John Madden

Sometimes I feel envious when my friends go to parties and I have to go to bed. But my friends always tell me that the parties really aren't that much fun anyway. Whatever I've missed, I've made up for. Most kids don't get to go to the Olympics and win three gold medals. It's definitely been worth it and I wouldn't do it if I didn't want to.

Janet Evans

What made me a champion? My father's coaching, training, and persistent encouragement paved the way. But it was something more: I was consistent over a long period of time because I never looked back, never dwelled on my defeats. I always looked ahead.

Chris Evert

As a kid, I always thought I was behind and I needed that extra hour to catch up. Jim Jones once told me, "No matter how many shots you take, somewhere there's a kid out there taking one more. If you dribble a million times a day, someone is dribbling a million and one." Whenever I'd get ready to call it a day, I'd think, "No. Somebody else is still practicing. Somebody—*somewhere*—is playing that extra ten or fifteen minutes and he's going to beat me someday." I'd practice some more and then I'd think, "Maybe that guy is practicing his free throws now." So I'd go to the line and practice my free throws and that would take another hour. I don't know if I practiced more than *anybody,* but I sure practiced enough. I *still* wonder if somebody—somewhere—was practicing more than me.

Larry Bird

WINNING!

I'm a firm believer that people only do their best at things they truly enjoy. It's difficult to excel at something you don't enjoy.

Jack Nicklaus

You've got to love what you're doing. If you love it, you can overcome any handicap or the soreness or all the aches and pains, and continue to play for a long, long time.

Gordie Howe

You always have to focus in life on what you want to achieve.

Michael Jordan

Ain't no man can avoid being born average, but ain't no man got to be common.

Satchel Paige

Nobody wants to be mediocre in life. The mediocre are the top of the bottom, or the best of the worst, or the bottom of the top, or the worst of the best.

Lou Holtz

Ability may get you to the top, but it takes character to keep you there.

John Wooden

W I N N I N G !

You are bound to have days when nothing goes right. The trick is to stay serene. The whole secret of mastering the game of golf—and this applies to the beginner as well as to the pro—is to cultivate a mental approach to the game which will enable you to shrug off the bad shots, shrug off the bad days, keep patient, and know in your heart that sooner or later you will be back on top.

Arnold Palmer

The big thing is not what happens to us in life, but what we do about what happens to us.

George Allen

Was my comeback worth it? Yes, it was, a million times over. I got to live out the greatest boyhood dream of all. I got to do what the experts said was impossible, to come back from cancer and pitch a major league game. Without a deltoid muscle in my pitching arm, I won a game in a pennant drive in front of thousands of screaming fans.

I've learned a lot in the past two years. I've learned how precious my wife and children are. I've learned how important it is to serve other people. Most of all, I've learned to put my life in God's hands. The hardest part has been the uncertainty. I had to learn to do what was in my grasp, one day at a time, leaving the rest trustingly to God.

Such are the lessons that come from facing adversity. I don't think I could have gained them in any other way.

Dave Dravecky

WINNING!

It's not whether you get knocked down, it's whether you get up.

Vince Lombardi

You never really lose until you stop trying.

Mike Ditka

Keep your head up; act like a champion.

Paul "Bear" Bryant

Many people in sports think of success and excellence as though they are the same. They're not.

Success is perishable and often outside our control. In contrast, excellence is something that's lasting, dependable, and largely within a person's control.

In sports, in business, in politics, we all know people who are very successful and who try to keep other people down. But people who truly excel don't resent excellence in others. People who shoot only for success, however, always feel threatened by other people's success.

Success is measured by what other people think: by whether they ask for autographs, buy tickets, stand up to applaud and cheer. Excellence is best measured by the achiever.

Joe Paterno

The way a team plays as a whole determines its success. You may have the greatest bunch of individual stars in the world, but if they don't play together, the club won't be worth a dime.

Babe Ruth

The secret of winning football games is working more as a team, less as individuals. I play not my eleven best, but my best eleven.

Knute Rockne

Success demands singleness of purpose.

Vince Lombardi

In order to be a leader, you have to know your job. You have to make people want to follow you, and nobody wants to follow somebody who doesn't know where he's going.

Joe Namath

A quarterback must take charge, he must be a leader. You have to be decisive. You must know what you want to do—and do it.

Johnny Unitas

Contrary to the opinion of many people, leaders are not born. Leaders are made, and they are made by effort and hard work.

Vince Lombardi

The secret of managing a club is keeping the five guys who hate you away from the five guys who haven't made up their minds.

Casey Stengel

Managing is like holding a dove in your hand. Squeeze too hard and you kill it; not hard enough and it flies away.

Tommy Lasorda

I hold it more important to have the players' confidence than their affection.

Vince Lombardi

I've earned respect thanks to basketball. And I'm not here just to hand it to the next person. Day in and day out I see people take on that challenge, to take what I have earned. I've got something that people want. And I don't ever want to give it away. Whenever the time comes when I'm not able to do that, then I'll just back away from the game.

Michael Jordan

When you step onto that field, you cannot concede a thing.

Gale Sayers

It's harder to stay on top than it is to get there.

Don Shula

A beginner does eight repetitions of a certain exercise with his maximum weight on the barbell. As soon as it hurts, he thinks about stopping. I work beyond that point.

Growing is something unusual for the body when you are over eighteen. The body isn't used to ten, eleven, or twelve reps with a maximum weight. Then I do ten or fifteen sets of this in a row. No human body was ever prepared for this and suddenly it is making itself grow to handle this new challenge, growing through this pain area.

The last three or four reps is what makes the muscle grow. This area of pain divides the champion from someone else who is not a champion. That's what most people lack, having the guts to go on and just say they'll go through the pain no matter what happens.

Arnold Schwarzenegger

If you're a gymnast something is always hurting, but you still train. You just have to learn to live with discomfort.

Mary Lou Retton

The man who can drive himself further once the effort gets painful is the man who will win.

Roger Bannister

All of us get knocked down, but it's the resiliency that really matters. All of us do well when things are going well, but the thing that distinguishes athletes is the ability to do well in times of great stress, urgency, and pressure.

Roger Staubach

Do not let what you cannot do interfere with what you can do.

John Wooden

Try not to do too many things at once; know what you want, the number one thing today and tomorrow. Persevere and get it done.

George Allen

Don't try to perform beyond your abilities—but never perform below them.

Frank Robinson

You are really never playing an opponent. You are playing yourself, your own highest standards, and when you reach your limits, that is real joy.

Arthur Ashe

You know, Bobby Knight probably had the best quote I've ever seen. He said, "You don't play against opponents—you play against the game of basketball." He's right. I don't play against opponents. I play against the game.

Larry Bird

Compete against yourself, not others.

Peggy Fleming

You can be out there in the middle of a tough match pleading to yourself, "Concentrate! Concentrate!" and it won't happen for you. Concentration is much more elusive than that.

The concentration you need has to come to you way before your match. Concentration is born on the practice court, alone with your groundstrokes, your foot speed, and everything else. You must mentally treat your practice sessions as matches, concentrating on every ball you hit. You must be keen, alert, and enthused, and as you cover all of your shots, thinking about just one thing at a time, you are making the mental process more and more automatic. This is what a true tennis craftsman achieves. A better quality practice creates a better quality match.

Martina Navratilova

An hour of hard practice is worth five hours of foot-dragging.

Pancho Segura

You play the way you practice.

Pop Warner

Concentration is why some athletes are better than others. You develop that concentration in training. You can't be lackadaisical in training and concentrate in a meet.

Edwin Moses

The only person I know who is stronger than I am—and more stubborn—is my mom. When I was growing up, she cleaned people's houses during the day and cleaned a motel at night. She also raised ten children. And people try to tell me that playing two sports is hard.

She said that when her supervisor came by, he could bounce a coin off the bed because she put everything she had into making that bed right. She told me that any room she cleaned, you could go in and give it the white-glove test, and your glove would come out clean. Her coworkers would ask her, "Why do you spend so much time making these rooms spotless?" and she'd say, " 'Cause that's the way I keep my house. That's the way I'm teaching my kids."

She wanted everything to be perfect. So do I.

Bo Jackson

Every day you waste is one you can never make up.

George Allen

It's what you learn after you know it all that counts.

John Wooden

I've never known a man worth his salt who in the long run, deep down in his heart, didn't appreciate the grind, the discipline. There is something in good men that really yearns for discipline.

Vince Lombardi

My talent is a gift of God—I am only what He made me. You need balance, and speed, and strength. But there is something that God has given me. It's an extra instinct for the game. Sometimes I can take the ball and no one can foresee any danger. And then, two or three seconds later, there is a goal. This doesn't make me proud, it makes me humble, because it is a talent that God gave me.

Pélé

Talent is God-given, be humble; fame is man-given, be thankful; conceit is self-given, be careful.

Anonymous (often quoted by John Wooden)

I wanted to be the greatest hitter who ever lived. A man has to have goals—for a day, for a lifetime—and that was mine, to have people say, "There goes Ted Williams, the greatest hitter who ever lived." Certainly, nobody ever worked harder at it. It was the center of my heart, hitting a baseball. I lived for my next turn at bat. If there ever was a man born to be a hitter it was me. As a kid, I wished it on every falling star: "Please, let me be the hitter I want to be."

Ted Williams

You have got to want to be the best before you can even begin to reach for that goal, and you have got to be prepared to sacrifice a lot to get there.

Billie Jean King

What athletics teaches is the self-discipline of hard work and sacrifice necessary to achieve a goal. Nowadays, too many young people are looking for a shortcut. They want a free ride, a handout. For guys who've been in athletics this shouldn't be true because they know what it takes. There are no shortcuts to success. Just the blood, sweat, and tears which produce results. Life is the same as athletics. You have to work to accomplish anything.

Roger Staubach

If a person believes he deserves success, he's got a shot at it. There's only one way I know to feel you deserve success, and that's if you work hard.

Lou Holtz

From the time I was very young, I realized how hard my father worked for a living in the gold mines, drilling all day long 10,000 feet underground. I grew up knowing you cannot be a success in life if you don't work very hard.

This lesson certainly applies to golf. I came into my chosen profession realizing the value of a stroke. I did not want to waste a single swing, knowing that it might make my future or break it. This is a very important attitude, one that all truly great players possess.

Lesser golfers never learn the full value of a stroke. There are a lot of fellows who have been given everything, or perhaps they have the gift of too much natural ability.

"What the hell, what's a shot?" you hear them say. They are mistaken. Each shot is important.

Gary Player

I used to get angry at myself for every mistake I made. I'd get so angry I'd lose my concentration and play badly for a few minutes before I'd get a grip on myself again. I still get angry at myself for mistakes, but I've learned to shake them off. You don't want to forget your mistakes. You want to learn from them. But the time to think of them is between games or in practice sessions. You've got to put your mistakes into a corner of your mind during games and go on applying yourself to the next play and the rest of the game.

Jerry West

The real champion puts silly errors or unlucky breaks out of his mind and gets on with the game.

Stan Smith

Preparation is everything. It is easy to say, "I am going to win," but it is hard to convince yourself that it is really possible. After all, the other racers are thinking the same thing. So I don't think about it; instead, I concentrate on my training and my equipment, which really determines who will make it. Then, on the day of the race, I can say with confidence, "I am ready."

Jean-Claude Killy

If I work on a certain move constantly, then, finally, it doesn't seem so risky to me. The move stays dangerous and looks dangerous to my foes, but not to me. Hard work has made it easy. That is my secret. That is why I win.

Nadia Comaneci

One of the more interesting compliments I've ever been paid came when somebody said that the best thing about me was that I wasn't afraid to look bad. Some guys are embarrassed when they are knocked down and absolutely mortified when they have a shot blocked. Over the years, I've had hundreds of shots blocked. You've got to go in and take chances.

John Havlicek

Hustle every shot, even the "impossible" ones. I should say especially the impossible ones, because if you make a point off one of those, you may deal a severe blow to your opponent's confidence.

Stan Smith

Sloppiness is a disease. Nobody ever built a great organization just worrying about the big things. It's the little things that give you the edge. If the equipment manager in the locker room doesn't check his equipment properly, the player senses it, the sloppiness gets into his bloodstream and the disease spreads. The important thing is to find people who are committed to detail and to standards of excellence.

Joe Paterno

The first thing is to know your faults and then take on a systematic plan of correcting them. You know the saying about a chain being only as strong as its weakest link. The same can be said of the chain of skills a man forges.

Babe Ruth

W I N N I N G !

John Havlicek came to us in 1962. He was a rookie on a pro team that had won the championship six years in a row. A team led by a big, intense black man named Bill Russell. One day after practice, soon after he arrived at camp, John mentioned that he was looking to buy a stereo and wondered where the best place would be. Russell heard this and the next thing John knew he was in Russell's car being chauffeured around town in search for the best deal. John couldn't get over it. Here was the superstar breaking his butt for the young rookie. This was the kind of thing that the rest of us on the team took for granted. It was Russell's way and it became the Celtics' way. John Havlicek learned that day that Celtics help one another off and on the court and that every man on the team is valued as a human being.

K. C. Jones

When I was a kid, I let too many opponents off the hook. I found out that you have to play with the intention of making it a short day, of doing the job quickly and thoroughly. I don't mean rush it. Anything but that. But when you have the opportunity, you strike.

Rod Laver

People don't seem to understand that it's a damn war out there. Maybe my methods aren't socially acceptable to some, but it's what I have to do to survive. I don't go out there to love my enemy. I go out there to squash him.

Jimmy Connors

I've learned that something constructive comes from every defeat.

Tom Landry

Losses are always a relief. They take a great burden off me, make me feel more normal. If I win several tournaments in a row, I get so confident that I'm in a cloud. A loss gets me eager again.

Chris Evert

I don't think we can win every game. Just the next one.

Lou Holtz

WINNING!

When I'm on the ice, I look for openings. That's what the game is all about. . . . Maybe I react to openings quicker than other players, I don't know for sure. But when I see something that looks open to me, I go. See you later.

Bobby Orr

In the last analysis, you make your own breaks—in golf as in life. Sure, you'll get some bad ones. But if you can roll with your misfortunes, if you can keep calm and optimistic, you'll get some good breaks, too.

Arnold Palmer

I swing big, with everything I've got. I hit big or I miss big. I like to live as big as I can.

Babe Ruth

The greatest asset any hitter can have is to be fearless at the plate. You can't be afraid of being hit and be a good hitter.

Rod Carew

Every great hitter works on the theory that the pitcher is more afraid of him than he is of the pitcher.

Ty Cobb

Fear is your best friend or your worst enemy. It's like fire. If you can control it, it can cook for you; it can heat your house. If you can't control it, it will burn everything around you and destroy you.

Cus D'Amato

The father of the Jesuits, Saint Ignatius, said we should live by a maxim that seems like a paradox. He said, "Always work as though everything depended on you. Yet always pray knowing that everything depends on God."

Over the years, that dynamite thought has exploded into something larger and larger in my life. It means to me now: Never be afraid to accept your own limitations or the limitations of others. Accept that we're all pretty small potatoes. Yet always know how great each of us can be. I never forget to remember that there's a higher power playing the biggest game of all—and that we small potatoes are only playing football. Yet I never forget to remember the first part of that maxim: Always work—or play—as though everything depends on you.

Joe Paterno

Larry Bird is one hell of a competitor. You can tell he is hurting, he's not running as well as he should, he's pulling back. But you say, "Larry, are you all right?" And he says, "Yeah," and goes out there and does his job. Those are the kind of guys you go across the river with, guys you go over the mountain with. I've never known another player so loyal. If you're Larry's teammate, you're one of the most important people in the world to him.

Kevin McHale

The difference between a successful person and others is not a lack of strength, not a lack of knowledge, but rather a lack of will.

Vince Lombardi

We all have an interior "comfort zone" that we want to be in. Picture a good club golfer playing Jack Nicklaus. His self-image is probably that he is a good golfer, but not good enough to beat Nicklaus. If he beat Nicklaus, he would be uncomfortable with the demands of his new self-image. So he does whatever he can to get back in that comfort zone, even if it means missing a two-foot putt on the 18th green.

In sailing, an average sailor who gets ahead of Lowell North or Dennis Conner in an important series will most likely do something careless in order to get behind. But once he gets behind he'll stick like glue, not lose another foot. You see people like this in every fleet. They are very hard to beat at the local level, but once at a major championship, they simply can't picture themselves winning.

Dennis Conner

WINNING!

My strongest point is my persistence. I never give up in a match. However down I am, I fight until the last ball. My list of matches shows that I have turned a great many so-called irretrievable defeats into victories.

Bjorn Borg

Another club can be beating you for six innings but for some reason the good ball clubs get tough and win them in the last three.

Billy Martin

Winners never quit and quitters never win.

Vince Lombardi

I don't kick lockers or throw bats the way some guys do. I think when you do that kind of thing, you can only eventually injure yourself and hurt your ball club. There's certainly no real personal satisfaction in an outburst like that. When things go wrong, I try to sit down and analyze what I did wrong and correct it next time. Normally there's an explanation for just about everything.

Jim Palmer

A man may make mistakes, but he isn't a failure until he starts blaming someone else.

John Wooden

When you're behind, the idea is to do something, but not everything. You want to get a flow going, then you can take a chance.

Joe Montana

The ballplayer who loses his head, who can't keep his cool, is worse than no ballplayer at all.

Lou Gehrig

I had no chance of controlling a ball game until I first controlled myself.

Carl Hubbell

For me, there's no purpose if you don't have a wife and kids; there's really no purpose to make money or be successful. I can't imagine being single and working so hard. Mostly I do it because I have a family. If I were single, I'd take things a lot easier. I'm racing and making a lot of sacrifices for my family, making sure we're going to have a nice life when I'm done with cycling. Without them, I know I wouldn't be nearly this successful.

Greg LeMond

I felt that my marriage had made me a better football player. I wasn't taking all those bruises only for myself. I had a happy family life, and it helped me go about my job.

Ray Nitschke

WINNING!

A man can be as great as he wants to be. If you believe in yourself and have the courage, the determination, the dedication, the competitive drive, and if you are willing to sacrifice the little things in life and pay the price for the things that are worthwhile, it can be done. Once a man has made a commitment to a way of life, he puts the greatest strength in the world behind him. It's something we call *heart power.* Once a man has made this commitment, nothing will stop him short of success.

Vince Lombardi

Be the best no matter what you do in life.

Walter Alston

I made up my mind a long time ago not to get too excited, no matter which way the crowd goes. I get paid for playing left field and for hitting that baseball. I am not a participant in a popularity contest.

Ted Williams

I never smile when I have a bat in my hands. That's when you've got to be serious. When I get out on the field, nothing's a joke to me.

Hank Aaron

I'm not concerned with your liking me or disliking me. . . . All I ask is that you respect me as a human being.

Jackie Robinson

If you have an objective in life, you shouldn't be afraid to stand up and say it. In the second grade, they asked us what we wanted to be. I said I wanted to be a ballplayer and they laughed. In the eighth grade, they asked the same question, and I said a ballplayer and they laughed a little more. By the eleventh grade, no one was laughing.

Johnny Bench

The most important thing that young athletes must do is to pick the right sport. Not one that they just like a little bit, but one that they love. Because, if they don't really love their sport, they won't work as hard as they should. Me? I loved to hit.

Babe Ruth

It's funny in the huddle sometimes: Every one of our receivers wants the ball, and they won't hesitate to say so. They'll tell me they can do this or that. That doesn't bother me at all. Of course, there are times when everyone is talking and time is running out, and I'll have to tell them to shut up. That's part of playing quarterback. But as a quarterback, you *want* to play with people who want the ball. It's the players who don't want it you have to worry about.

Dan Marino

If there's something that has to be done to win a game, I've always thought I could do it. Obviously, there have been times when I've failed. But I haven't thought that I was going to fail. I've always thought that I could do what was necessary.

Michael Jordan

What is absolutely indispensable is strict follow-through, effort, and stick-to-itiveness. Don't be frightened if things seem difficult in the beginning. That's only the initial impression. The important thing is not to retreat; you have to master yourself. This ability to conquer oneself is no doubt the most precious of all the things sports bestows on us.

Olga Korbut

My attitude is never to be satisfied, never enough, never. The girls, they must be little tigers, clawing, kicking, biting, roaring to the top. They stop for one minute—poof!—they are finished.

Bela Karolyi

The one unbreakable rule about hitting is this: If a batter hits well with his particular stance and swing, think twice—or more—before suggesting a change.

Stan Musial

The stupidest thing in the world is a man with his own gifts trying to act like someone else. You can be taught, and you can be inspired. But you've still got to be you.

Willie Mays

Forget about style; worry about results.

Bobby Orr

When I was twelve, I was throwing my racket all over the place and cheating all the time. I was a real nut case. Hitting balls over the fence—everything. My parents were ashamed and finally refused to come to a single match.

Suddenly I was suspended for six months by the Swedish Association. I lived in a very small town and the news of my suspension spread quickly. People whispered behind my back. I took it very much to heart and it was devastating. I remember as if it were yesterday.

Now if my opponent cheats, or if I get a terrible call, I don't say a thing. I guess the memories have stuck with me so that I'll never do anything crazy or unsportsmanlike in front of a lot of people. I'd hope I wouldn't do it anywhere, crowd or not.

Bjorn Borg

I still get nervous before every game. I don't think you'd be normal if you didn't get the chills. I still do. You want to do well. I have a fear of failure. That's motivation in itself.

Joe Montana

No matter how long you have been playing, you still get butterflies before the big ones.

Pee Wee Reese

If you're not just a little bit nervous before a match, you probably don't have the expectations of yourself that you should have.

Hale Irwin

What is your goal? To be president of your company? Top salesman? A teacher or professor with tenure? Take it from a guy who knows: Those are all good and worthy goals, but they won't bring you what you want and need. True success and happiness does not come from material things and dreams coming true. It comes only from knowing God.

There's nothing wrong with achieving. A person who belongs to God should strive for nothing but excellence. But set your sights on eternal things, not material.

Joe Gibbs

It doesn't matter who wins or loses, you pray, "Thy will be done."

George Foreman

There are few things you can't do as long as you're willing to apply yourself. There are many times I wish I was playing eighteen holes of golf instead of training in miserable cold weather. But in the final analysis, I'd rather win the Tour de France than play eighteen holes of golf. That's why I do it.

Greg LeMond

If you're going to be a champion, you must be willing to pay a greater price than your opponent.

Bud Wilkinson

Working hard becomes a habit, a serious kind of fun. You get self-satisfaction from pushing yourself to the limit, knowing that all the effort is going to pay off.

Mary Lou Retton

John Wooden believed in supreme conditioning and unwavering fundamentals, not only knowing which plays to run and how to run them but being capable of calling up the physical and emotional stamina at the precise time you need it to win. Application is his guiding light, being tired all the time, accepting whatever pain is necessary in order to achieve your goal.

Mr. Wooden would drill us fiercely and expect dedication; he accepted no less. His philosophy was that if you needed emotion to make you perform then sooner or later you'd be vulnerable, an emotional wreck, and then nonfunctional. He preferred thorough preparation over the need to rise to an occasion. Let others try to rise to a level we had already attained; we would be there to begin with.

Kareem Abdul-Jabbar

There are scores of players who can hit every shot in the book who never make it into a Grand Slam event. Those who make it are there because they are mentally tougher: They *wanted* it more.

John McEnroe

Two people are in the same business on the same street. One of them prospers and the other does not. Why? Because one of them wants it more than the other. It is not always the strongest man who wins the fight, or the fastest man who wins the race, or the best team that wins the game. In most cases it is the one who wants it the most, the one who has gone out and prepared, who has paid the price.

Tommy Lasorda

The more success one achieves, the more pressure there is that goes with it, and I accept it. I'd sure rather have the pressure of success than the lack of pressure that goes with anonymity.

Roger Clemens

I know this will come as a shock to a lot of people but I have dined in the homes of the rich and the mighty and I have never once kicked dirt on my hostess. Put me on the ball field, and I'm a different man. If you're in professional sports, buddy, and you don't care whether you win or lose, you are going to finish last. Because that's where those guys finish, they finish last. *Last.*

Leo Durocher

Failure is not fatal, but failure to change might be.

John Wooden

When you make a mistake, there are only three things you should ever do about it: 1) admit it; 2) learn from it; and 3) don't repeat it.

Paul "Bear" Bryant

A winner never whines.

Paul Brown

You prove your worth with your actions, not with your mouth.

Pat Riley

It is said that good things come to those who wait. I believe that good things come to those who work.

Wilt Chamberlain

I have always adhered to two principles. The first is to train hard and get into the best possible physical condition. The second is to forget all about the other fellow until you face him in the ring and the bell sounds for the fight.

Rocky Marciano

However good or bad I'm feeling, none of it touches my racing. I won't let it. I just turn it off. I've learned to control my mind that way.

Bobby Unser

They don't give you points for worrying.

Bob Mathias

Negative attitudes are a sort of poison.

Fran Tarkenton

Having what some folks would call my cowboy life to go back to when I'm not playing baseball is probably one of the things that accounts for my longevity. Working with cattle, hunting, fishing, being in the great Texas outdoors is a perfect release for me after the pressure of baseball season.

I think that's one reason I've played so long—I keep the game in its place. I never take the game home with me. And I believe I've lasted this long as a power pitcher because I'm a real strong believer in conditioning. I don't smoke or drink anything stronger than an occasional beer, and I watch what I eat, but most important, I'm dedicated to my conditioning program all year round. Some players don't seem to have the dedication. I like to work out, and I set aside time for doing it and never let anything interfere.

Nolan Ryan

WINNING!

You hit home runs not by chance, but by preparation.

Roger Maris

My idea was to do everything better than anybody else ever had. I concentrated on every aspect of the game.

Willie Mays

To be an innovator, you can't be worried about making mistakes.

Julius Erving

To give yourself the best possible chance of playing to your potential, you must prepare for every eventuality. That means practice. Now I know that very often you "just don't have the time." In spite of that, if you really want to improve, you will have to make the decision, and then the commitment. There are no shortcuts. You must lay the proper foundation.

Seve Ballesteros

It is easy to fall into slovenly habits in golf, and those habits fasten on a fellow and stick like burrs. Don't be slovenly. Do everything right. Don't hurry a shot, and when you make it, execute it the very best you know how.

Walter Hagen

While I'm practicing I am also trying to develop my powers of concentration. I never just hit the ball. I decide in advance how I want to hit it and where I want it to go.

Try to shut out everything around you. Develop your ability to think only of how and where you want to hit the shot you are playing.

An ability to concentrate for long periods of time while exposed to all sorts of distractions is invaluable in golf. Adopt the habit of concentrating to the exclusion of everything else while you are on the practice tee and you will find that you are automatically following the same routine while playing a round in competition.

Ben Hogan

WINNING!

I began playing baseball with other kids in my neighborhood when I was about ten years old. In those days I preferred anything to working on my father's fishing boat or cleaning it up when the fishing day was over. I hated the smell, that was all. My father, on the other hand, looked on baseball, which he knew very little about, in much the same way as I did fishing.

We did not play on fancy-cut diamonds with base paths and grass. We played on a cleared space of ground we called "Horse Lot" because it was used by a dairy firm as a parking area for its horse-drawn milk wagons. Most of the time the spectators at our games were horses. We used rocks for bases and most of us played barehanded because we could not afford baseball gloves. The rest of our equipment consisted of an old ball, held together by bicycle tape, and an oar handle for a bat.

Joe DiMaggio

W I N N I N G !

You can't get much done in life if you only work on the days when you feel good.

Jerry West

A pro plays whether he wants to or not.

Carl Yastrzemski

You can't let problems lick you, because they will always be there.

George Allen

Everyone is dealt a problem in life. Mine is missing four fingers.

When I was little, my parents always encouraged me to be outgoing. My dad was always pushing me, when I'd see someone new, to walk up to the kid, shake his hand and say, "Hi, my name is Jim Abbott." My dad never wanted me to be held back because of my hand.

Jim Abbott

Boys must learn that the one thing that is important is their self-respect. Keep your self-respect and you win. Lose your self-respect and you are defeated, no matter how the world looks at you.

Red Grange

If you play an aggressive, hustling game, it forces your opponents into errors.

Pete Rose

As a manager, I ask only one thing of a player—hustle. If a player doesn't hustle, it shows the club up and I show the player up. Hustle is the only thing I really demand. It doesn't take any ability to hustle.

Billy Martin

Give me some scratching, diving, hungry ballplayers who come to kill you.

Leo Durocher

I have never gone on a ballfield and given less than my level best.

Hank Aaron

You just have to play for yourself. For your own pride and self-respect.

Dick Butkus

I put the most pressure on myself because of my ambition to be the best basketball player ever. What happens around me can't put any more pressure on me than that.

Julius Erving

Once you've been around sports long enough, you see how success softens some performers. To stay on top you have to develop an attitude that excellence is always defined as wanting to do better. When you understand what it takes to sustain championship form, then complacency is something that isn't part of your life. You don't allow it.

Pat Riley

Rarely will you see an athlete who hasn't put on ten or fifteen pounds over a full career, but even rarer are the ones who don't put on the same amount of mental fat. That's the biggest killer of aging champions, because concentration and mental toughness are the margin of victory.

Bill Russell

You have to want to do it yourself. If you're the kind of guy who has to be primed every week for every game, you aren't going to stay in the league very long.

Johnny Unitas

It's important to be a self-starter. Nobody is going to wind you up in the morning and give you a pep talk and push you out. You have to have a firm faith and belief in yourself.

Lou Holtz

I've always felt it was not up to anyone else to make me give my best.

Akeem Olajuwon

WINNING!

To win you have to risk loss.

Jean-Claude Killy

Home-run hitters strike out a lot.

Reggie Jackson

If you don't dream, you may as well be dead.

George Foreman

Throughout my life, from childhood through my career in the major leagues, I've always believed I was going to get a hit. *Every* time up. It has never made any difference to me who is pitching. I want that pitcher to *feel* the confidence I have at the plate; I want every pitcher to know that I'm the best there is and that when I step into the batter's box, he's got his hands full.

Rod Carew

The difference between the possible and the impossible lies in a man's determination. Set your goals in life, and go after them with all the drive, self-confidence, and determination that you possess.

Tommy Lasorda

I understand that people consider me a great athlete and I appreciate that. But when writers ask me, "What does it feel like to be one of the greatest players in hockey history?" I don't know what to say. I guess it's just embarrassing. If anything, I think about how to avoid being special. The last thing I want is a limo while the rest of my teammates have to ride the bus. The last thing I want is the fanciest suite or the nicest table when I'm with the team.

It's like the time Gordie Howe was playing in the WHA. He was in his forties then, a legend, and he went up to the coach and said, "Did you have a bed check last night?" The coach said yes. "Well, why didn't you check my room? I'm part of this team, too."

That's the kind of thing I admire.

Wayne Gretzky

The first requisite of the good hitter is confidence. No player can be a hitter without it. Relax—be yourself up at the plate. Such advice had been handed down to me by fellows who knew what they were talking about—Cobb, Lefty O'Doul, Cronin, Ruth. If there is fear in your heart that the pitcher might hit you, you might as well give up baseball. There are lots of pitchers who deliberately aim one close to your body to scare you away from the plate. That's all part of the game.

Joe DiMaggio

I don't think any man, or athlete, thrives on pressure. You survive pressure and rise above it, even conquer it, if you're good enough.

Reggie Jackson

I warm up for every match believing that I'm going to win. To some, that may sound cocky. I think it is the result of having confidence in my game.

I'm not talking about going into a match simply telling yourself, convincing yourself, that you'll win. If you do that, all you're building is a phony confidence. Your opponent will probably shoot it down quicker than he can pick off a short defensive lob.

What you should be after is the real thing. And there's only one way to build that kind of confidence. That is to practice often enough and long enough. Deep down inside, you've got to know that you're capable.

Jimmy Connors

If you've got enough enthusiasm so it infects other people, everybody's going to do better, and the fans are going to come out to see you.

Willie Mays

Enthusiasm is everything.

Pelé

If you are not fired with enthusiasm, you will be fired with enthusiasm.

Vince Lombardi

I'm a totally different person on the mound than I am on the street. The casual country gentleman, if that's what I could be called, wouldn't get anybody out in the big leagues. At that level you have to be single-minded, focused, and tough. I mean really tough. You've got to go after the hitters, take every advantage you can, work on their weak spots, and want to beat them. There's no playing around. Anybody who's ever been on a big league mound knows that you're always one pitch from failure.

Nolan Ryan

I'm not out there just to be dancing around. I expect to win every time I tee up.

Lee Trevino

Each year, I set out to hit at least one point higher, drive in one more run, and belt one more home run than the previous season. I always strive to be better.

Wade Boggs

I always leave home plate thinking about an extra base. If I have a cinch double, I'm always thinking triple. If I have a cinch single, I'm always thinking double.

Pete Rose

It isn't hard to be good from time to time in sports. What's tough is being good every day.

Willie Mays

To meet my goals, I couldn't let up when I was playing tennis. "Don't ever try to be nice and give them a game," my coach always said. "If you can beat them love-and-love, then beat them love-and-love. You have to be tough from the beginning. Get out there and get it over with as quickly as you can."

Tracy Austin

I always have good finishes. You go as hard as you can until the end. You can always rest when it's over.

Janet Evans

Whatever you do, don't do it halfway.

Bob Beamon

Baseball's 90 percent mental. The other half is physical.

Yogi Berra

Hitting is concentration. Free your mind of everything. Study the flight of the ball from the pitcher.

Reggie Jackson

A full mind is an empty bat.

Branch Rickey

WINNING!

When I take the mound to throw the first pitch, I expect to throw a perfect game. If I give up a walk, I intend it to be the only walk in the game. If I give up a hit, then my goal is to throw a one-hitter. But I don't allow my mind to stray that far ahead. My one and only priority is the next pitch, not the no-hitter, the shutout, or even the out. If every pitch is thrown with the right mechanics and is rooted in sound strategy, and if my regimen has put me in proper condition, the results will take care of themselves.

Orel Hershiser

Somebody's gotta win and somebody's gotta lose—and I believe in letting the other guy lose.

Pete Rose

There are some sailors who don't work hard on their boats and gear, and I think it's because they are looking for excuses to lose. They may blow a series when a piece of gear breaks, or their sails or keel may not be just right. They can always blame their loss on their equipment. It may be that those guys really *want* to lose. But somebody like Lowell North or myself will be comfortable with himself only if he works hard on his equipment. A guy content with third because he can say that the top two crews won only because they worked harder is comfortable with himself. His self-image is that of a person who could be the best in the world "if only." Once you get to the point when you honestly feel that you have done everything within your power to win and have given yourself no excuse to lose, you're really going to be hard to beat.

Dennis Conner

WINNING!

The trouble with being number one in the world is that it takes something of a driving, perfectionist mentality to attain that position in the first place, so that once you achieve number one, you don't relax and enjoy it. Once you become number one, your main thought is to protect that, to get better still, to stay ahead of number two. It's unfortunate, but almost by definition, if you are the best, if you are the champion of the world, you can't take much pleasure in it—or otherwise you couldn't be the best.

Billie Jean King

Nobody remembers who finished second but the guy who finished second.

Bobby Unser

W I N N I N G !

For about two weeks, every boy who had tried out for the basketball team at my high school knew what day the cut list was going to go up. We knew it was going to be posted in the gym. In the morning. So that morning we all went in there, and the list was up. We stood there and looked for our names. If your name was on the list, you were still on the team. If your name wasn't on the list, you were cut. Mine wasn't on the list.

I looked and looked for my name. I looked at the H's, and the I's, and the J's, and the K's, and I wasn't there, and I went back and started again. But I wasn't there.

I went through that day numb. I sat through my classes. I had to wait until after school to go home. That's when I hurried to my house and closed the door to my room and I cried so hard. It was all I wanted—to play on that team.

Michael Jordan

I have come to really believe that the people who make it in the world aren't the most talented ones or the smartest or the luckiest, or necessarily the bravest. The ones who make it are the dogged ones. Just plain tenacity. Those are the ones who take the jolts and get up and look at the sky.

Fran Tarkenton

Thousands of touchdowns, hundreds of games and championships have been saved by players refusing to give up and finally making the big play. No matter how many times you're blocked, you must get up again and again and never stop until the last sounds of the whistle have died away.

Dick Butkus

I ski to win. When the day comes that I can't get myself into a fighting mood anymore, I won't be able to win and I'll stop racing.

Ingemar Stenmark

I've still got that competitive drive when I'm on the field. If I lost that, I'd quit real quick, because I'm convinced you can't survive without it. You can lose a little of your physical power and compensate with drive, but without drive it doesn't make any difference what kind of ability you have. You're not going to get far until you have a burning desire to excel.

Nolan Ryan

Any team can be a miracle team. The catch is that you have got to go out and work for your miracles. Effort is what ultimately separates journeymen players from impact players and one-year champs from the teams of lasting greatness. It might be the effort spent since schoolboy days, taking a few dozen extra shots after practice, building habits that will pay off throughout a career. It might be the effort at any one very crucial moment in a tight game. Great effort springs naturally from a great attitude.

Pat Riley

Winning is not a sometime thing; it's an all-time thing.

Vince Lombardi

I don't believe in team motivation. I believe in getting a team prepared so it knows it will have the necessary confidence when it steps on a field and be prepared to play a good game. Players can sense this and respond to it.

It's a long year and there are a lot of highs and lows. Sometimes it's difficult to get ready to play, but if they are not ready, they know it. If you can cause them to be ready, and be prepared for all situations they'll have to face, they'll be motivated.

Tom Landry

To win at all, a team has to be obsessive about the fundamentals and little things.

Joe Gibbs

I was brought up by my parents and by others not to smile and tell jokes on the court, but to be very serious. To be on the court meant to concentrate.

John McEnroe

When you walk on the court, clear your mind of everything unrelated to the goal of playing the match as well as you can.

Stan Smith

The worst thing you can do is start slow, or con yourself into thinking that you can take your time getting into a match. The curtain is up so you've got to perform.

Jack Kramer

The first thing I do after losing, regardless of whether I lost a close one because of a silly lapse or simply was snowed under by a rival running on a hot streak, is to forget it. I take a look at my calendar and start thinking about where we'll be playing next week, and I'll show 'em then!

Nancy Lopez

Sure you feel better and you sleep better when you win. But there's nothing you can do about a game that is over. You can't change it. You can replay it as many times as you want, but the score is always the same. All you can do is learn from it and look ahead to tomorrow.

Walter Alston

Strength is not nearly as important as desire. I don't think you can teach anyone desire. I think it's a gift. I don't know why I have it, but I do.

Larry Bird

Every time your back is against the wall, there is only one person that can help. And that's you. It has to come from inside.

Pat Riley

To see a man beaten not by a better opponent but by himself is a tragedy.

Cus D'Amato

Desire is the most important factor in the success of any athlete.

Willie Shoemaker

Desire! That's the one secret of every man's career. Not education. Not being born with hidden talents. Desire.

Bobby Unser

You have to be a dedicated person. You have to want to do it more than anything else. You have to want to be number one. Then you have to have the ability.

Mario Andretti

WINNING!

I play to win, even when common sense should tell me that I no longer have a chance. Even when I have been playing at my worst, or when all the breaks have been going against me, I approach each new day, each new hole, as a glorious opportunity to get going again.

Arnold Palmer

How badly do I want to win? If I were playing third base and my mother was rounding third with the run that was going to beat us, I would trip her. Oh, I'd pick her up and I'd brush her off, and then I'd say, "Sorry, Mom." But nobody beats me!

Leo Durocher

I'll admit I gave in to the fatigue during some games, and I'd be out there just going through the motions. That's when I could count on it. *Whack!* A loud noise, and pain would shoot upward from my kidneys. I'd glower at the other center. A few plays later, *Whack!* It would happen again. After a few more whacks, I'd be beating the other center to death with the basketball. I'd forget that I was tired. But once in awhile, if I were lucky, I'd turn around after a whack quickly enough to see that it was not the other center who was hitting me, but sneaky little K. C. Jones, my own teammate! "Well, you weren't doing nothing out there," he'd say, "so I had to get your attention." And we'd laugh.

Bill Russell

If you find you can push someone around, then you push him around.

Gordie Howe

The pitcher has to find out if the hitter is timid. And if the hitter is timid, he has to remind the hitter he's timid.

Don Drysdale

When you have someone in trouble, you have to put him away. If you don't you'll just give him a shot of confidence and he'll come back and knock your head off. Anybody who has competed in any sport, or in life, will tell you that.

Dick Butkus

Watch Chris Evert or Tracy Austin and you will see the killer instinct at work. They play every point all out, regardless of their lead, and refuse to give their opponents a chance to breathe life into their own chances. What hurt me early in my career was this lack of purpose. It was common for me to be up 6–0, 5–1, and proceed to ease things up. I would think I had the match won, lose my concentration, or feel sorry for my opponent, and suddenly I'd be involved in a tie-breaker to decide the third set. That's where the killer instinct shines. Killer instinct gives you the power to finish the match. When you've got someone down, killer instinct will tell you to beat them and get off the court.

Martina Navratilova

I don't think I'm the most popular guy on the field. That's all right. I don't want them to love me. No one ever sees me smile or pat an opponent on the back and say, nice play. Why should I? He's the enemy. For those sixty minutes I hate him. If he's made a good play, so what? He's supposed to make them. He's a pro. That's what he gets paid for. Why should I encourage him to make more? It'll only hurt me and my team. When a guy puts a block on me, I want to kill him not congratulate him.

Dick Butkus

Nobody who ever gave his best regretted it.

George Halas

Go out that door to victory!

Knute Rockne

I can't stress too much the importance of shoving the last point right out of your mind. Forget it. A point won't come back no matter how much you think about it. If you played it badly there's no way you can reverse it; if you played it well, it won't help you get the next point.

The next point—that's all you must think about. "Gotta get the next point!" is what you tell yourself. "Gotta get the next point."

Rod Laver

Keep your mind on the game. You can't get mentally lazy. When you do, you get hurt. You have to concentrate.

O. J. Simpson

I believe that if you are bored with life, your problem is that you don't have a lot of goals. You must have goals and dreams if you are ever going to achieve anything in this world.

Lou Holtz

Many people flounder about in life because they do not have a purpose, an objective toward which to work.

George Halas

Success doesn't carry a dollar sign. . . . Success isn't something that just happens. Success is learned. Success is practiced. And then it's shared.

Sparky Anderson

If I had my career to play over, one thing I'd do differently is swing more. Those 1,200 walks I got, nobody remembers them.

Pee Wee Reese

To be good, a race driver has to take chances. The guy who has confidence and pushes it to the limit, that's the real race driver.

Mario Andretti

Never let up. The more you can win by, the more doubts you put in the other players' minds the next time out.

Sam Snead

After we beat Ohio State last year, I could have said, "Hey, we won the Big Ten championship. We're going to the Rose Bowl." But our second half was awful. We gave up thirty-one points. So I chewed them out. "THIS GAME WAS NOT GOOD ENOUGH FOR CHAMPIONS!" I said.

On the other hand, during the Rose Bowl, at half-time, we were losing to USC 14–3. In the locker room, I did not speak of mistakes. I did not scream about a lousy first half. I simply said, "We can beat this team." I knew we could. We made the adjustments. And we won.

That's a key to motivation. When your team is winning, be ready to be tough, because winning can make you soft. On the other hand, when your team is losing, stick by them. Keep believing.

Bo Schembechler

Age is a question of mind over matter. If you don't mind, it doesn't matter.

Satchel Paige

I don't give a damn about age. I can still do the job.

George Blanda

When you're going up against the best, you've got to give it your best.

Kareem Abdul-Jabbar

Determination that just won't quit—that's what it takes. There have been many times, late in a race, when I felt beat, but I never fully accepted it until it was over, until the checkered flag dropped. I always have it in mind that something might happen, some miracle, to get me in the winner's circle. And there have been times when something did happen and I won a race nobody gave me a chance of winning.

A. J. Foyt

Breakthroughs occur. If you have a positive attitude and constantly strive to give your best effort, eventually you will overcome your immediate problems and find you are ready for greater challenges.

Pat Riley

I play hard, I play in pain because I want to pour it out for the team. . . . When you've been playing the game all your life you realize the ultimate compliment comes from your teammates, the fellows with whom you not only play but also share both the good and bad times. When the game is over I just want to look at myself in the mirror—win or lose—and know I gave it everything I had, that I didn't let anyone down. That's my number one priority. I want to know that I played the game straight from the heart.

Joe Montana

There's no better tonic for an injured hockey player than scoring a goal.

Bobby Hull

Some guys play with their heads. That's okay. You've got to be smart to be number one in any business. But more important, you've got to play with your heart—with every fiber of your body. If you're lucky enough to find a guy with a lot of head and a lot of heart, he's never going to come off the field second.

Vince Lombardi

Hustle isn't a God-given talent, like quick feet. It's something that a person develops through sheer will. It's a state of mind. Every coach in the world, from the pros to the youth leagues, prays for his players to develop more hustle.

Pat Riley

Building a basketball player is like building anything else—you start with the foundation. If the foundation is solid, the rest will be more solid.

Jerry West

The key to success is to learn to do something right. Then do it right every time.

Pat Riley

Failure to prepare is preparing to fail.

John Wooden

I demand total involvement from our players. After God and family, the only thing that's important is what the Dolphins do on game day. That requires total involvement. If there are any statements that I don't ever want attributed to me, they are: "Our opponents wanted the game more than we did," or "They were more ready to play the game than we were," or "Their emotions ran higher than ours."

Don Shula

The selfish player is the worst, like a cancer; a few of them can quickly devastate a football team. I wanted players who blocked for other runners and didn't worry how many times they carried the ball.

Paul Brown

Golf's like everything else in life: You get out of it what you put into it. I proved that to myself again in 1979, my worst year since turning pro. At the time I thought I was preparing fully for each tournament I entered, but in retrospect, I realize that the effort wasn't quite 100 percent. I worked at the game, but I didn't work hard enough. Perhaps subconsciously, after twenty-five years of being pretty successful at golf, I thought I could get by on natural talent plus experience. I proved to myself embarrassingly that I couldn't. Confidence is the most important single factor in this game, and no matter how great your natural talent, there is only one way to obtain and sustain it: work. That can be a hard fact to swallow, but doing so is the first step to excellence.

Jack Nicklaus

I suppose it's just human nature, but we all have the tendency to practice the things that we already do pretty well. In truth, we should do just the opposite if we hope to improve.

Nancy Lopez

It's easy to practice something you're already good at, and that's what most people do. What's tough is to go out and to work hard on the things that you don't do very well.

Pete Rose

Practice without improvement is meaningless.

Chuck Knox

You should practice with a purpose. Personally, it would really frustrate me to practice for three or four hours in the morning, walk away, and two hours later say to myself, "Gee, I wish I had worked a little harder on this or that." It's the quality of the time you spend practicing that counts, not the length of time.

Jimmy Connors

One secret of Jack Nicklaus's greatness is that he never seems to hit a practice shot that he doesn't take as seriously as the shot on the last hole of a major championship. He's never careless with a practice shot, never hits balls without a purpose.

Tom Watson

Show me a good and gracious loser and I'll show you a failure.

Knute Rockne

If you don't invest very much, then defeat doesn't hurt very much, and winning isn't very exciting.

Dick Vermeil

When you win you get a feeling of exhilaration. When you lose you get a feeling of resolution. You resolve never to lose again.

Vince Lombardi

I met Cassius Clay at the station when he moved to Miami and took him to his chosen one-room apartment in the cheapest part of town. He didn't have to stay in such a joint, there were expenses to cover his accommodation, but he had a pal sharing his room and Cassius really didn't mind where he stayed. He was in Miami to train, to fight, to win, and to become a champion. Where he slept was incidental as long as it didn't interfere with his objectives.

I realized there was a lot to learn about this young man. When I arrived at the gym he was always there, ready to go. When our training session was over he was the last to leave. There was always an extra minute on the speed bag, or the heavy bag. Boxing demands dedication, and invariably it pays off. Cassius Clay is proof of that.

Angelo Dundee

Most people think football is strictly a muscle game. In the pros, though, every club is loaded with so much power that sheer strength is canceled out. You've got to outsmart the other team to win, and that takes enormous concentration on details.

Frank Gifford

You can take the best team and the worst team and line them up and you would find very little physical difference. You would find an emotional difference. The winning team has a dedication. It will have a core group of veteran players who set the standards. They will not accept defeat.

Merlin Olsen

If the coach is organized, everything falls into place. If he has self-discipline, the team has discipline. If he's dedicated, the team is dedicated. Everything revolves around the head coach. He's the one who has to make the team go.

Ray Nitschke

The strength of the group is the strength of the leader. Many mornings when I am worried or depressed, I have to give myself what is almost a pep talk, because I am not going before that ball club without being able to exude assurance. I must be the first believer, because there is no way you can hoodwink the players.

Vince Lombardi

One of the great things about baseball is that it helps you submerge your own private aims in a team effort to win. It gets so you actually forget your own hurts at times, so strong is the desire to help your club—the men you work and play with every day—come out on top. Even Ty Cobb, who was supposed to have been the most individualistic of them all and who had many a row with his teammates, still, according to men who knew him, was ready to risk a broken leg any time to help his club come out first. Babe Ruth and Joe DiMaggio too had this ability to submerge themselves in the team effort to come out on top and both of them played ball with sore arms and bad legs when they felt the club needed them.

Mickey Mantle

You never get ahead of anyone as long as you're trying to get even with him.

Lou Holtz

Problems are the price you pay for progress.

Branch Rickey

Fatigue makes cowards of us all.

Vince Lombardi

It's easier to back away from excellence than it is to give everything you've got. It's easier to let the frustrations and distractions and fatigue of the long season erode your performance. But it's not satisfying in the long run.

Pat Riley

I will demand a commitment to excellence and to victory, and that is what life is all about.

Vince Lombardi

A leader is interested in finding the best way—not in having his own way.

John Wooden

A group called Gifts, Inc., arranged for me to meet an eleven-year-old boy named Rusty. Rusty had leukemia, and his wish was to meet me. He told me he also wished I would win the Heisman Trophy. I wished I could have taken him hunting or fishing or swimming. I wished I could have shown him how to get in trouble, doing the things kids are supposed to do. It's so sad to see that kids like Rusty don't get a chance to see what the world is really like. Hospitals and needles and chemotherapy and doctors and nurses—that's all they know.

Rusty helped me keep the Heisman in perspective. I wanted to win it, but if I didn't, I still had my health, I still had my family. There are so many things more important than honors and awards.

Bo Jackson

W I N N I N G !

I don't get a big charge out of being the leading scorer. The object of competing is winning. I just try to do what has to be done for us to win. That might be anything at any time—defense, rebounding, passing. I get satisfaction out of being a team player.

Kareem Abdul-Jabbar

Passing the ball is what I like best, because if I can get the ball to a guy and he scores and I see the gleam in his eye when he's running back down the court, it's the greatest feeling in the world.

Larry Bird

When I'm playing basketball, I'm playing to win, nothing else. Not to score, to rebound, or to excel in one particular area of the game, but to win. That means I'm a rebounder, a scorer, a passer, even a cheerleader.

It means I'm going to be an example to my teammates of what having a winning attitude is all about.

It means I'll have an attitude of unselfishness that keeps me craving for more championships for my team, not glory for myself.

It means I'll set an example at every practice by practicing longer and harder than anybody else.

It means I'll challenge myself, I'll set goals.

It means I'll think "we," and not "me," every time I step onto the court.

Magic Johnson

Everybody judges players different. I judge a player by what he does for his ball club and not by what he does for himself. I think the name of the game is self-sacrifice.

Billy Martin

The most important measure of how good a game I'd played was how much better I'd made my teammates play.

Bill Russell

Individual commitment to a group effort—that is what makes a team work, a company work, a society work, a civilization work.

Vince Lombardi

ACKNOWLEDGMENTS

Special thanks to Vince Lombardi, Jr., and the Curtis Management Group (for use of photo, page 33), Carl Seid and The National Baseball Hall of Fame and Museum, Inc. (page 88), The Bettmann Photo Archive / UPI and Reuters Photo Libraries (pages 11, 22, 55, 66, 77, 110, 143), AP Worldwide Photos (pages 44, 132), The Sporting News Publishing Co. (page 99), and All-Sport Photography USA, Inc. (page 121). All quotations by and photos of Vince Lombardi copyright © 1993, Estate of Vince Lombardi under license authorized by Curtis Management Group, Indianapolis, Indiana, USA.

ABOUT THE AUTHOR

Michael Lynberg is the author of three previous books: *The Path with Heart*, *The Gift of Giving*, and *50 Simple Things You Can Do to Save Your Life*, which he coauthored with the UCLA School of Public Health.